MW00911295

A Special Gift
For

From

Date

Copyright © 1993
Brownlow Publishing Company,
6309 Airport Freeway,
Fort Worth, Texas 76117

All rights reserved. The use or
reprinting of any part of this book
without the express written permission
of the publisher is prohibited.
ISBN: 1-877719-70-6
Printed in Singapore

Hope

Edited by Paul C. Brownlow

Brownlow

Brownlow Publishing Company, Inc.

✌

Little Treasures
Miniature Books

FROM FRIEND TO FRIEND

GOLDEN MOMENTS—
Hope & Inspiration from
Leaves of Gold

PRECIOUS PROMISES

TREASURES FROM THE PSALMS

DEAR TEACHER

QUILTED HEARTS—*When Friends Are Near Hearts Abound in Love*

MOTHER—*A Little Book of Inspiration*

FOR MY SECRET PAL

ANGELS OF FRIENDSHIP—*Gather Half Their Joy*

FAITH—*All Things Are Possible to Those Who Believe*

HOPE—*If Hope Were Not Heart Would Break*

LOVE—*Love and You Shall Be Loved*

Contents

CHAPTER ONE ❧ 8

CHAPTER TWO ❧ 26

CHAPTER THREE ❧ 41

CHAPTER FOUR ❧ 62

CHAPTER FIVE ❧ 79

Great Hopes

You cannot put a great hope
into a small soul.

JENKIN LLOYD-JONES

*I*t has been said that man can live
about forty days without food,
about three days without water,
and about eight minutes
without air—but only
one second without HOPE.

ANONYMOUS

*H*ope well and have well.

PROVERB

Remember your word to your servant, for you have given me hope. My comfort in my suffering is this: Your promise preserves my life.

PSALM 119:49, 50

Those who would have nothing to do with thorns must never attempt to gather flowers.

ANONYMOUS

Using Life

What a difference it makes
when we are using life
rather than having life use us.
When we, to a marked degree,
are managing our moods,
controlling our emotions,
making life meaningful,
filling every day with
the heights of Christian living,

we may say with confidence
that we are using life.

But when worry grips the mind
and paralyzes the heart,
or the dull edge of sin robs life
of radiancy, or fear grips our life,
rather than an abiding faith,
and life runs out into a morass of
doubt, disillusionment, and despair,
we know that life is using us.

FRANK A. COURT

It is certainly wrong
to despair;
and if despair is wrong
hope is right.

JOHN LUBBOCK

Every minute life begins
all over again.

THOMAS MERTON

*L*earn from yesterday,
live for today,
hope for tomorrow.

ANONYMOUS

*H*e has delivered us
from such a deadly peril,
and he will deliver us.
On him we have set our hope
that he will continue
to deliver us.

1 CORINTHIANS 1:10

A Wish for Hope

May hope, thy pilot,
safely steer
Thee through all dangers
far or near!

*H*ope is the feeling that you will
succeed tomorrow in what
you failed at today.

ANONYMOUS

It is impossible for that man
to despair who remembers that his
Helper is omnipotent.

JEREMY TAYLOR

$\mathscr{G}$od puts the excess of hope in one man in order that it may be a medicine to the man who is despondent.

H. W. Beecher

$\mathscr{H}$ope deferred makes the heart sick; but when dreams come true at last, there is life and joy.

Proverbs 13:12

In One Tree

I looked up and saw a squirrel jump
from one high tree to another.
He appeared to be aiming for a
limb so far out of reach that
the leap looked like suicide.
He missed—but landed, safe and
unconcerned, on a branch several
feet lower. Then he limbed
to his goal, and all was well.

An old man sitting on the bench said,
"Funny, I've seen hundreds of 'em

jump like that, especially when there are dogs around and they can't come to the ground. A lot of 'em miss, but I've never seen any hurt in trying." Then he chuckled. "I guess they've got to risk it if they don't want to spend their lives in one tree."

I thought, "A squirrel takes a chance—have I less nerve than a squirrel?"

Since then, whenever I have to choose between risking a

new venture or hanging back,
I hear the old man
on the park bench saying,
"They've got to risk it if they don't
want to spend their lives in one tree."

So I've jumped again and again.
And in jumping I've learned why the
squirrels so often do it: it's fun.

OSCAR SCHISGALL

*H*e who has health has hope, and
he who has hope has everything.

ANONYMOUS

*T*he great pleasure in life is doing
what people say you cannot do.

WALTER BAGEHOT

*T*here are no hopeless situations,
there are only hopeless men.

CLARE BOOTHE LUCE

Just for One Day

Anyone can carry his burden,
however hard, until nightfall.
Anyone can do his work,
however hard, for one day.
Anyone can live sweetly, lovingly,
purely, till the sun goes down.
And this is all that
life really means.

ROBERT LOUIS STEVENSON

Accumulate Hope

It is just as easy to become
bankrupt in hope as to
become bankrupt in money.
Hope is a mixture. It is made
up of equal parts of courage,
work, will, and faith.
Inoculate your system with
these things and hope
will hover about you,
lead you on and defend you.
Accumulate hope.

CHAPTER TWO

Anchor of the Soul

Hope is like the sun, which, as we
journey toward it, casts the shadow of
our burden behind us.

S. SMILES

He who plants a tree plants a hope

LUCY LARCOM

Cling to Hope

No vision and you perish;
No ideal, and you're lost;
Your heart must ever cherish
Some faith at any cost.

Some hope,
some dream to cling to,
Some rainbow in the sky,
Some melody to sing to,
Some service that is high.

HARRIET DU AUTERMONT

This Alone

To suffer woes which
Hope thinks infinite;
To forgive wrongs darker
than death or night;
To defy Power,
which seems omnipotent;
To love, and bear; to hope
till Hope creates
From its own wreck
the thing it contemplates;

Neither to change,
nor falter, nor repent;
This, like thy glory,
Titan, is to be
Good, great and joyous,
beautiful and free;
This is alone Life, Joy,
Empire, and Victory.

Percy Bysshe Shelley

*W*hen you say a situation or a person
is hopeless, you are slamming the
door in the face of God.

CHARLES L. ALLEN

*A*ll we can do is to make the best of
our friends, love and cherish what
is good in them, and keep out
of the way of what is bad.

THOMAS JEFFERSON

Today well lived makes yesterday
a dream of happiness and every
tomorrow a vision of hope.

ANONYMOUS

But as for me, I will always have
hope; I will praise you more and more.

PSALM 71:14

While there is life there is hope.

LATIN PROVERB

Tomorrow

If we might have a second chance
To live the days once more,
And rectify mistakes we've made
To even up the score.
If we might have a second chance
To use the knowledge gained,
Perhaps we might become at last
As fine as God ordained.

But though we can't
retrace our steps
However, stands the score,
Tomorrow brings another chance
For us to try once more.

FARR

Probably nothing in the world arouses more false hopes than the first four hours of a diet.

DAN BENNETT

Greet the unseen with a cheer.

ROBERT BROWNING

The hope of life returns with the su

LATIN PROVERB

*F*or in this hope we were saved.
But hope that is seen is no hope at all.
Who hopes for what he already has?
But if we hope for what
we do not yet have,
we wait for it patiently.

ROMANS 8:24, 25

*G*reat hopes make great men.

PROVERB

In Your Hand

What is that you hold in your hand?
Nothing, you say? Look again.
Every hand holds some special gift—
A hammer, a broom, a pen,
A hoe, a scalpel, an artist's brush,
A needle, a microscope,
A violin's bow, a way with words

In the giving of faith and hope.
What is that you hold in your hand?
Whatever your gift may be,
It can open your door
to abundant life—
You hold in your hand the key.

HELEN LOWRIE MARSHALL

We are not perfectly free
until we live in pure hope.

THOMAS MERTON

The time I live in
is a time of turmoil,
my hope is in God.

FREDERICK THE GREAT

We have this hope as an anchor
for the soul, firm and secure.

HEBREWS 6:19

*E*verything that is done in the world
is done by hope. No husbandman would
sow one grain of corn if he hoped not it
would grow up and become seed;
no bachelor would marry a wife if he
hoped not to have children;
no merchant or tradesman would set
himself to work if he did not hope to
reap benefit thereby.

MARTIN LUTHER

CHAPTER THREE

The Singing Bird

Keep a green tree in your heart
and the singing bird will come.

CHINESE PROVERB

There is not enough darkness in all
the world to put out the light
of one small candle.

ANONYMOUS

Broken Hopes

As the tree is fertilized
by its own broken branches
and fallen leaves, and grows
out of its own decay, so men and
nations are bettered and improved
by trial, and refined out of broken
hopes and blighted expectations.

F. W. ROBERTSON

Find rest, O my soul, in God alone;
my hope comes from him.

PSALM 62:5

There is no medicine like hope,
no incentive so great,
and no tonic so powerful
as expectation
of something tomorrow.

O. S. MARDEN

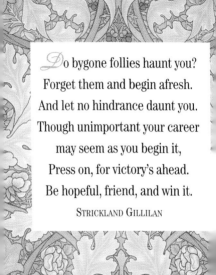

Do bygone follies haunt you?
Forget them and begin afresh.
And let no hindrance daunt you.
Though unimportant your career
may seem as you begin it,
Press on, for victory's ahead.
Be hopeful, friend, and win it.

STRICKLAND GILLILAN

*H*ope is the parent of faith.

CYRUS AUGUSTUS BARTOL

*N*ow the God of hope fill you
with all joy and peace in believing,
that ye may abound in hope,
through the power
of the Holy Ghost.

ROMANS 15:13

Be strong!
We are not here to play,
to dream, to drift;
We have hard work to do,
and loads to lift;
Shun not the struggle—
face it; 'tis God's gift.

Be strong!
Say not, "The days are evil.
Who's to blame?"
And fold the hands and acquiesce—

oh shame!
Stand up, speak out,
and bravely, in God's name.

Be strong!
It matters not how deep
entrenched the wrong,
How hard the battle goes,
the day how long;
Faint not—fight on!
Tomorrow comes the song.

MALTIE DAVENPORT BABCOCK

*H*ope proves man deathless.
It is the struggle of the soul,
breaking loose from
what is perishable,
and attesting her eternity.

HENRY MELVILLE

*T*ake short views,
hope for the best,
and trust in God.

SYDNEY SMITH

Eternity is the divine
treasure house,
and hope is the window,
by means of which mortals
are permitted to see,
as through a glass darkly,
the things which God is preparing.

WILLIAM MOUNTFORD

A Certain Hope

Command those who are rich
in this present world
not to be arrogant nor
to put their hope in wealth,
which is so uncertain,
but to put their hope in God,
who richly provides us with
everything for our enjoyment.

1 TIMOTHY 6:17

Meaning of Life

I looked more widely around me,
I studied the lives
of the masses of humanity,
and I saw that, not two
or three, or ten, but hundreds, thousan
millions, had so
understood the meaning of life
that they were able
both to live and to die.

All these men were well acquainted
with the meaning of life
and death, quietly labored,
endured privation and suffering,
lived and died,
and saw in all this,
not a vain,
but a good thing.

LEO TOLSTOY

In the lottery of life there are more prizes drawn than blanks, and to one misfortune there are fifty advantages. Despondency is the most unprofitable feeling a man can indulge in.

DeWitt Talmage

I live in hope and that I think do al who come into this world.

Robert Bridges

The proper function of man is to live, not to exist. I shall not waste my days in trying to prolong them. I shall use my time.

JACK LONDON

To be seventy years young is sometimes far more cheerful and hopeful than to be forty years old.

OLIVER WENDELL HOLMES

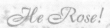

He died!
And with Him perished
all that men hold dear;
Hope lay beside Him
in the sepulcher,
Love grew corpse cold, and
all things beautiful beside,
Died, when He died!

He rose!
And with Him hope arose,
and life and light.
Men said, "Not Christ, but Death,
died yesternight.
And joy and truth and
all things virtuous
Rose, when He rose."

AUTHOR UNKNOWN

*H*ope, like faith,
is nothing if it is not courageous:
it is nothing if it is not ridiculous.

THORNTON WILDER

*H*ope arouses,
as nothing else can arouse,
a passion for the possible.

WILLIAM SLOANE COFFIN, JR.

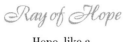

Ray of Hope

Hope, like a
gleaming taper's light,
Adorns and cheers our way;
And still, as darker
grows the night,
Emits a brighter ray.

OLIVER GOLDSMITH

Those Who Hope

He gives strength to the weary and
increases the power of the weak.
Even youths grow tired and weary,
and young men stumble and fall;
but those who hope in the Lord
will renew their strength.
They will soar on wings like eagles;
they will run and not grow weary,
they will walk and not be faint.

ISAIAH 40:29-31

"*Totally without hope
one cannot live.*"
To live without hope is to cease
to live. Hell is hopelessness.
It is no accident that above
the entrance to Dante's hell
is the inscription:
"*Leave behind all hope,
you who enter here.*"

FEODOR DOSTOEVSKI

CHAPTER FOUR

If Hope Were Not

If hope were not,
heart would break.

ANONYMOUS

Always be prepared to give an
answer to everyone who asks you to gi
the reason for the hope that you have

1 PETER 3:15

I Shall

I shall wear laughter on my lips
Though in my heart is pain—
God's sun is always
brightest after rain.

I shall go singing
down my little way
Though in my breast
the dull ache grows—

The song birds come again
after the snows.

I shall walk eager still
for what Life holds
Although it seems
the hard road will not end—
One never knows the beauty
round the bend!

Anna Blake Mezquida

*H*ope is the pillar that
holds up the world.
Hope is the dream of a waking man.

PLINY THE ELDER

*B*ut the eyes of the Lord are on
those who fear him, on those whose
hope is in his unfailing love.

PSALM 33:18

*H*e who lives in hope
dances without a fiddle.

To improve the golden moment of
opportunity and catch the good
that is within our reach
is the great art of life.

JOHNSON

Of all the forces that make
for a better world,
none is so indispensable,
none so powerful, as hope.
Without hope men
are only half alive.

CHARLES SAWYER

Whispering Hope

Soft as the voice of an angel,
Breathing a lesson unheard,
Hope with a gentle persuasion
Whispers her comforting word:
Wait till the darkness is over,
Wait till the tempest is done,
Hope for the sunshine tomorrow,
After the shower is gone.

ALICE HAWTHORNE

Don't let life discourage you;
everyone who got where he is
had to begin where he was.

RICHARD L. EVANS

What can be hoped
for which is not believed?

AUGUSTINE

His pleasure is not in
the strength of the horse,
nor his delight in
the legs of a man;
the Lord delights in
those who fear him,
who put their hope
in his unfailing love.

PSALM 147:10, 11

*I*f you observe a really happy man
you will find him building a boat,
writing a symphony, educating his son,
growing double dahlias in his garden,
or looking for dinosaur eggs in the
Gobi desert. He will not be striving for
it as a goal itself. He will have become
aware that he is happy in the course of
living life twenty-four hours of the day.

W. BERAN WOLFE

Hope, Child

Hope, child, tomorrow
and tomorrow still,
And every tomorrow hope;
trust while you live.
Hope, each time the dawn
doth heaven fill,
Be there to ask as God
is there to give.

VICTOR HUGO

The sunshine smiles upon
the winter days of my heart,
never doubting
of its spring flowers.

RABINDRANATH TAGORE

There are those who cast
their bread upon the waters,
hoping it will be returned to them
toasted and buttered.

ANONYMOUS

Hope and Joy
and Life

Make me too brave
to lie or be unkind.
Make me too understanding,
too, to mind
The little hurts
companions give,
and friends,
The careless hurts
that no one quite intends.

May I forget
What ought to be forgotten,
and recall,
Unfailing, all
That ought to be recalled,
each kindly thing,
Forgetting what might sting.
To all upon my way,
Day after day,
Let me be joy, be hope!
Let my life sing!

DAVIES

Inspired by Hope

We continually remember
before our God and Father
your work produced by faith,
your labor prompted by love,
and your endurance inspired
by hope in our Lord Jesus Christ.

1 THESSALONIANS 1:3

The Window Sill

Every morning lean thine arms awhile
Upon the window sill of heaven
And gaze upon thy Lord.
Then, with the vision in thy heart,
Turn strong to meet thy day.

AUTHOR UNKNOWN

CHAPTER FIVE

Travel in Hope

To travel hopefully is better than to arrive.

SIR JAMES JEANS

Beautiful Hope

Every day is a fresh beginning,
Every morn is the world made new.
You who are weary
of sorrow and sinning,
Here is a beautiful hope for you—
A hope for me
and a hope for you.

Every day is a fresh beginning;

Listen, my soul,

to the glad refrain,

And, spite of old sorrow

and older sinning,

And puzzles forecasted

and possible pain,

Take heart with the day,

and begin again.

SUSAN COOLIDGE

Golden Town

They say that life is a highway
and its mile-stones are the years,
And now and then there's a toll-gate
where you buy your way with tears.

It's a rough road and a steep road,
and it stretches broad and far,
But at last it leads to a golden Town
where golden Houses are.

JOYCE KILMER

I rise before dawn and cry for help;
I have put my hope in your word.
My eyes stay open through the
watches of the night,
that I may meditate
on your promises.

PSALM 119:147, 148

*H*ope proves a man deathless.

HERMAN MELVILLE

The hopeful man sees success
where others see failure,
sunshine where others
see shadows and storm.

O. S. MARDEN

The word which God has written
on the brow of every man
is Hope.

VICTOR HUGO

Hope for a Better World

We cannot hope to build

a better world

without improving

the individual...

toward this end,

each of us must work

toward his own
highest development,
accepting...his share
of responsibility
in the general life
of humanity.

MARIE CURIE

The heart bowed down
by weight of woe
to weakest hope will cling.

ALFRED BUNN

The future...seems to me no
unified dream but a mince pie,
long in the baking,
never quite done.

E. B. WHITE

Never live in hope or expectation
with your arms folded.

ANONYMOUS

I pray also that the eyes
of your heart may be enlightened
in order that you may know the hope
to which he has called you.

EPHESIANS 1:18

A New Chapter

Life is a journey and not a home;
a road, not a city of habitation.
And the enjoyments and blessings
we have along the way are but
little inns on the roadside, where we
may be refreshed for a moment,
that we may with new strength
press on to the goal...

Every worthwhile accomplishment,
big or little, has its stages of
drudgery and triumph; a beginning,
a struggle, and a victory.

A few wise friends with whom
to counsel, a few good books to read
and absorb, and with courage
and faith we are well equipped
for the facing of life's difficulties.

and disappointments, as well as its
pleasures and successes.
Lives are made of chapters.
After one is written
it cannot be revised,
but we can write a new chapter
with each new day.

PHILLIPS BROOKS

Be Hopeful

Be hopeful, friend, when clouds are
dark and days are gloomy, dreary,
Be hopeful even when the heart
is sick and sad and weary.
Be hopeful when it seems your plans
are all opposed and thwarted;
Go not upon life's battlefield
despondent and fainthearted.

And, friends, be hopeful of yourself.

Do bygone follies haunt you?

Forget them and begin afresh.

And let no hindrance daunt you.

Though unimportant your career

may seem as you begin it,

Press on, for victory's ahead.

Be hopeful, friend, and win it.

STRICKLAND GILLILAN

*M*ay integrity and uprightness
protect me, because
my hope is in you.

PSALM 25:21

*H*ope means expectancy
when things are otherwise hopeless

G. K. CHESTERTON

*H*ope is life and life is hope.

ADELE SHREVE